"*Healing Words from Mary* allows us to step realistically into the mysteries of the rosary, to experience with Mary, with Joseph, with Jesus, the depth of human emotion that wound its way through their lives. Through the reflections of Mary, we find less mystery and more in common with our own journeys through life. Mary shows us the struggles her family faced being rejected by friends who didn't care to understand. She shows us the worries of parents when their teenage children become too independent or decide to leave home. We hear Mary speak of the helplessness she felt when she was unable to alter the course of someone else's pain. Her overwhelming joy as she hugged Jesus after the resurrection gives us a hopeful glimpse into our own eternal future.

"*Healing Words from Mary* would best be read and prayed one mystery at a time, not read cover to cover all at once. We cannot appreciate the depth of emotion and personal insight that Mary shares through the pen of Isaias Powers unless we take the time to mingle our similar emotions with hers. Pray these words gently and find in them a reflection of your own joyful, sorrowful, and glorious moments."

Richard G. Furey
Author, *Mary's Way of the Cross*

"Both the title, *Healing Words from Mary,* and the subtitle of this very inspiring little book, *Entering the Mysteries of the Rosary,* truly tell the reader what to expect. Its timely meditations on the traditional 15 mysteries are structured into 'Mary Speaks to You,' 'Prayers to Mary,' and 'Prayers for Others.' This format is superbly well-suited for listening to the memories and prayerful reflections of Mary about her Son's saving mysteries.

This inspiring book should help the attentive reader to relate much more intimately with the 'real' Mary. It not only enriches our praying of the rosary but also leads us toward a deeper and deeper union with Mary's Son."

Fr. Frederick M. Jelly, O.P.
Author, *Madonna: Mary in the Catholic Tradition*

"*Healing Words From Mary* deals with the mysteries of the rosary. It devotes a section to each of the 15 mysteries. But Father Powers, in his infinite wisdom and infinite charm, has added three new decades. 'I wanted to feature the patience of Mary and Joseph as the extra joyful mystery,' he says, 'the patience of Mary as she returned to the upper room after the crucifixion as an extra sorrowful mystery, and, as the extra glorious mystery, the patience of Mary and Andrew at Pentecost after Peter told them both to quiet down.'"

*Catholic Twin Circle*

"The prayers in these pages suggest ways to start our own personal outpouring of personal prayer. In the introduction, the author reminds us that there are very few words in the gospels that are called Mary's own. Yet, here she has long, often tender conversations, as if she's sitting in your kitchen having a little chat with you. This little book will help to keep the reader close to Mary in the month of May and through the rest of the year."

*Today's Catholic*

"Just when you might think that nothing new or original can be written about the mysteries of the rosary, Father Powers, a veteran author of spiritual books, treats us to his version of the fifteen mysteries. In this treatment, Powers opens each chapter with the scriptural background, then he presents a 'conversation' with the Blessed Mother in which she "speaks to us." He concludes with a Marian prayer and a prayer for others."

Msgr. Charles Dollen
*The Priest* magazine

"*Healing Words From Mary* is a book with a unique new idea: hearing Mary's 'words' in the mysteries of the rosary—mysteries which the author cites as framework for grappling with the basic questions of life, whether or not one has always been devoted to Mary."

*Crux of the News*
Clarity Publishing

# ISAIAS POWERS

# Healing Words from Mary

### Entering the Mysteries of the Rosary

## TWENTY-THIRD PUBLICATIONS
Mystic, CT 06355

**Second Printing 1997**

Twenty-Third Publications
185 Willow Street
P.O. Box 180
Mystic, CT 06355
(860) 536-2611
800-321-0411

ISBN 0-89622-702-2
Library of Congress Catalog Card Number 96-60655
Printed in the U.S.A.

# Contents

# Glorious Mysteries

# Healing Words from Mary

# Introduction

To read *Healing Words from Mary,* it is not necessary that you already love Mary or pray the rosary. It helps if you do, but it is not necessary. To benefit from this book the only essential condition is that you have thought seriously about what life means, what love's consequences are, how friendships happen, where we go after we die, how we should take the words of Jesus to heart . . . thoughts like these.

If you have puzzled over such considerations, Blessed Mary has too. And she can help you with your own moments of gladness, sorrow, and perplexity.

There are two big advantages to this book. One I call the "Hallmark grabber." You know how people like to browse through the aisles of greeting cards. They have an anniversary to commemorate, a cause to share, a love to link up with, a day to give thanks for. They want to say Happy Birthday, Happy Graduation, or Happy Secretaries Week. They want to say something, but they need a boost to begin the process. So they look and look. Finally, they find a card that has the phrase or illustration that says it for them. The thoughts on the card become the surrogate statement of *their* thoughts, or it is the launch for saying what they want to add by way of personal postscript. The prayers in these pages will serve the same purpose. They suggest ways to begin your own reflections and start you off with your out-pouring of personal prayer.

The other advantage of this book is the "two-pronged prayer." Aside from Mary's healing words to you in each chapter, there are also sections called "Prayer to Mary" and "Prayer for Others." It has been my experience (perhaps yours too) that my intercessions sometimes focus complete-ly on other people, as I consider both global problems and local and family needs. At other times I become very per-sonal in my petitions; my own neediness is so pervasive that I become the only one I have in mind in my prayer.

Well, the prayers of this book include both categories. This way you don't have to be concerned that "I'm praying only for myself." And no one will become smug and think, "Other people fill up my prayers, and I nobly ignore my own concerns!" The truth is that *both* are important: prayer for others and for ourselves. You will find a place for both in these pages.

You may be surprised that Mary has so much to say in what follows. We have very few words in the gospels that can be called "Mary's own." Yet here she has long, often tender, conversations, as if she is sitting in your kitchen, having a little chat with you. Her utterances are sometimes words of consolation, sometimes practical connections about contemporary affairs, and sometimes vivid memo-ries about her own joys, sorrows, and glories. The only hon-est explanation of why Mary has so much to say in this book is that, as I was writing, it only seemed right for her to do so.

You will notice that there is one extra joyful, sorrowful, and glorious mystery. I wanted to feature the patience of Mary and Joseph as the extra joyful mystery, the patience of Mary as she returned to the upper room after the crucifixion as an extra sorrowful mystery, and, as the extra glorious mystery, the patience of Mary and Andrew at Pentecost after Peter told them both to quiet down.

As you will see, patience figures strongly in these meditations. The importance of patience and the vital connection of prayer to our ordinary lives—these are the standout qualities of the book.

I shall pray for all who read these pages, which were my prayers first. And I thank you for being so patient with me.

# Joyful Mysteries

# The Annunciation

The angel Gabriel was sent from God to a virgin whose name was Mary. He said to her, "Rejoice, most highly favored daughter; the Lord is with you." [The angel continued:] "The power of the Most High will overshadow you."

Luke 1:28, 35

[Just before he ascended into heaven, Jesus said to his disciples:] "Wait . . . until you are clothed with power from on high."

Luke 24:49

## Mary Speaks to You

Thank you for praying the rosary. You honor me. You celebrate how dear you are to me. Everyone, of course, is dear to me. But you are especially dear because we are linked together by the mysteries of love that I pondered over and over, centuries ago. And now you are doing the same thing. Just as the Angel Gabriel commanded me to rejoice, I command the same from you.

Yes, rejoice. Be joyful! The rosary begins with the very message God gave me. This kind of joy has nothing to do with bubbling-over bliss. Real joy can exist side-by-side with sorrows and setbacks. Godlike joy is a disposition, allowing the Lord to love you *his way*.

Of course, I know it's not always easy to accept the gift and the *command* of joy. Misfortunes can argue against even its possibility. Bad experiences with people who have been hostile or irritable or demanding—these can interfere with normal happiness or peace. Many different kinds of situations can scuttle all hope for security.

You can feel ruined by someone's mismanagement of funds, a natural disaster disrupting your life, the death of a dear one . . . even having a temperature or losing sleep could induce you to argue with the angel Gabriel . . . who, this very moment, might want to tell you: "Rejoice! You are favored by God. The Lord is with you!" This is a message that most people, most of the time, consider too good to be true.

For a moment, I thought so too. When I was told to be full of joy, my immediate instinct was to back away. Before I had a chance to really think about it, I reacted with reasons why I could *not* rejoice. Something inside me started to click off certain items of difficulty I could complain about . . . if I wanted to. "How can I rejoice?" I could have said, "with this head cold lasting for two weeks! When Rebecca, my neighbor, snubbed me at the well this morning! When I'm so worried about how much longer I can keep up the house now that my mother and father have died! When my cousin hasn't spoken to me for two years! When my classmates ridicule me because I take my religion seriously! When the heavy rains of last week ruined the seamless garments I just made!" Things like that. What I mean to say is that I had as many reasons for not being happy as anyone has. Things weren't perfect in my life either.

I resisted the temptation to air my gripes. Prayer helped me to wait quietly until I could understand the angel's promises. My faith assured me that God is a God of love, who wants happiness for all the world. I had no business making things difficult for God. This was the most important lesson I learned on the morning of the annunciation. There is one more too: Joy doesn't depend on the accidents of nature or the various reactions of individuals. It depends on God. God is the one who has favored me. God likes me . . . and loves me. *That's* why I had to be happy.

Because God was with me—and always would be—no

one or nothing could take away my confidence. Gabriel spoke the truth and I agreed with it.

And so my life with my son began. I said yes to God's plan of love, letting everything develop as it would. And see how well it all turned out? Now I have joy to the full.

Such a gift is yours as well. God favors you and wants you to accept the plan of love for you. My constant prayer to God is that joy may bless every day of your life, including all eternity. I pray this on your behalf and on behalf of all the people you care about.

### *Prayer to Mary*

Thanks, Mary, for reminding me about this. It's so easy, sometimes, to become discouraged, to let mean-hearted people and bad-luck situations make me unhappy. It seems that my capacity for joy is the first thing to go. Why do I allow people and circumstances to control me so?

Let me have some of your serenity, my Lady. Help me to understand my value. If Jesus promised all his disciples that the "power of the Most High will overshadow them"— his words include me too. The gift of the Spirit at Pentecost means that I've been given the same favor you received at the annunciation. The power of God, the energy of the Holy Spirit, has filled me. I have dignity like yours, Mary; I have a connection to the divine. No matter what I feel like at any time—whether luck abandons me or people reject me— God has favored me by the gift of Jesus.

Stay with me, Blessed Lady. Help me to keep my courage up. No matter what the setbacks, the fears, or the hurts may be, let me hear God's message as a bell ringing to awaken me to my most profound awareness. Whether I *feel* like it or not, I *must* rejoice because I am highly favored, because the Lord is with me. Amen.

### Prayer for Others

Blessed Mary, look with love on the people I pray for now:

*(Here, mention the names and the circumstances of those who are discouraged with life, upset about their meager pay or ill health, resentful because others have hurt them or ignored them, depressed by bad working conditions or mean fellow workers, unhappy because of sickness, addicted to a compulsive habit.)*

Reach out to them, Mary, with your maternal love. Help them to understand how much God loves them and will continue to love them, long after all their hardships and hurt feelings have come to an end.

Let them know goodness once again, dear Mother. Replace the rehearsal of their woes with confidence that God loves them, and that others love them too. Let them feel more joy. Let them agree to live more agreeably with themselves until they can accept what you accepted when Christianity began: when they and I, like you, can really hear the message that God is with us.

Strengthen the people that I pray for until they are no longer afraid of anything. Let them once again find God and learn that they can, and must, rejoice. Amen.

# The Visitation

Mary promptly left Nazareth and traveled to the hill country of Judea. She greeted Elizabeth. Then Elizabeth exclaimed, with full voice, "Blessed are you among women and blessed is the fruit of your womb! The moment you greeted me the baby in my womb danced for joy!"

Luke 1:39–56

### *Mary Speaks to You*

It is such a joy to have someone good to talk to. My cousin Elizabeth was that for me, as I was for her. I hope you and I can have the same kind of friendship.

Elizabeth and I didn't see each other often. Traveling was not as easy then as it is now. But our friendship was always alive. You have friends like that, I'm sure. It could be a year, or more, since you last met; yet you both respond as if you were together the day before. That's how it was at this second joyful mystery of mine. It is "mystery" because of the God-work connected to my child and hers. It was no mystery from the standpoint of friendship or the need for friendship. Everyone needs to tell her story and to be understood.

Oh yes, we certainly needed each other. I couldn't talk to anyone about the secret growing inside my womb. Who would believe me? A virgin getting big with child? Even Joseph had to wait—and it was weeks!—before the angel came to reassure him.

So I was all alone with this marvelous good news. Elizabeth was too. Who would believe that a woman her age was pregnant? Poor Zachary, her husband, was made mute because he didn't believe it. So there was no one to really share her excitement or hear her version about what happened, about her wonderful baby.

Then we met. I want you to take special notice of how generous we both were in "giving way" to the other. Elizabeth was just bursting with her news. I was bursting with mine. Even so, after we hugged each other, I didn't take over the scene with the story of the Word of God made flesh in me. I waited for my cousin to speak. She was older; I was in her house. Those eyes of hers were sparkling with happiness and eagerness . . . her big smile and everything about her spoke of a wonderful secret that just had to get out.

She did begin to speak first, but it was not about herself and her baby. It was in praise of my child and her pride in me, her happiness for me. I then did the same for her.

I hope you have a friend like Elizabeth—a friendship like ours. If you don't have one, or think you don't, you have to be one first. Sometimes, it seems like it's ten times harder to listen than it is to talk. Love isn't always easy. It has two gifts that must be nurtured: you have to be a good listener and you have to develop the instinct to know when to praise the one you're listening to. These gifts, the very stuff of love, are what Elizabeth and I cherished. They will be the source of joy for you as well.

### Prayer to Mary

Blessed Mary, let me share your friendship skills. Sometimes I talk far too much, heedless of the needs of others. I become so fixated on my own worries and setbacks that I don't even notice anyone else, or care whether they might have troubles too. Sometimes I'm so pepped up by my own good news, I go on and on about myself.

Mary, I really blunder in this matter of kindly conversation. Help me to manage this fault, to let prudence modify my enthusiasm. Teach me to be more courteous to my friends, show them more attentiveness, and be more sensitive in the way I tell stories. I want to be more like you and Elizabeth with the friends I have—allowing them to speak up first, being quick to praise and slow to blame . . . and slower, still, to express complaints.

As you rejoiced for your cousin because of the child within her, and as she did the same for you, so let me honor the goodness within those who bless me by their association.

And Mary, may I always rejoice because you are my friend, and I am yours. Amen.

### *Prayer for Others*
Blessed Mary, I now ask you to do everything you can to help:

*(Here, mention friends, certain members of your family, people at work who give you a hard time—all those who frustrate, anger, or disappoint you because they won't listen to you. Without judging them, simply mention them by name and tell Mary the circumstances of your difficulty.)*

Please, Mary, understand the tension I feel about these obstacles to friendship. I admit they are mutual obstacles. Please touch them—and me—with your loving care. I don't blame them for their behavior or presume to know their motives. I'm just saying that I feel bad because they seem to be too preoccupied to notice me, too tired to listen to me, too bored with life to bother about me, or too angry because I hurt them in the past.

Whatever the reason for our lack of friendship, I'd like it to change. I'd like to know them better, to work with them more smoothly. I want to enjoy shared respect and dignity as you and Elizabeth did.

Please heal the situation, Mary. Help them, and us, and it. Amen.

# Joseph and Mary, Patient with Each Other

## Extra Joyful Mystery

Joseph did not want to bring public shame to Mary, so he thought about quietly leaving her. Then, one day, an angel appeared to him in a dream and said, "Do not be anxious any longer. Take Mary to be your wife. That which is begotten in her is from the Holy Spirit."          Matthew 1:18–25

### Mary Speaks to You

I want to add one more joy to my joyful mysteries. I hope you will pray it with my husband and me. Call it Meditation on Patience; call it Relief That Comes, Thanks to Calmness; call it The Secret of Marital Bliss and the Glue of Any Good Friendship. It is all of these.

Joseph and I were upset, of course. Especially Joseph. What an ordeal he went through. Imagine living with these two undeniable facts: My fiancée is pregnant. And not by me!

What would you have done under the circumstances? Indeed, what have you done when someone has hurt you with facts not nearly so devastating as the ones Joseph was saddled with? Most people think Joseph had his dream on the same day he discovered those facts. Not so. Many weeks passed by before God's messenger told Joseph how I became pregnant and why. I couldn't tell him. It was not up to me to interfere in God's work. Besides, how would he believe such a miracle could take place unless the Miracle Worker told him?

So there we were, in Nazareth, in a quandary: What to do

with each other? How would we survive this threat to our love and friendship? Thank God we made it a *quiet* quandary. I am so glad that Joseph was not a lesser man. Someone else would have publicly denounced me, falling in with the town gossips. Or he might have issued an ultimatum, telling me, with righteous indignation, that he'd have no more to do with me.

You know how that happens to people. It may have happened to you. So you can imagine how I would have reacted to his rejection. I would have let my own self-righteous temper get the better of me. I would have blurted out how misunderstood I was . . . and how it wasn't my fault . . . and how *dare* he doubt me. I would have retaliated with "If that's how little you trust me, then go away." Things like that.

Oh, how glad we were that neither of us acted out of our hurt feelings. If we did, how could my child have grown up, and how could I have kept going, without Joseph's support and love? God blessed our patience, for it was only patience that got us through those weeks of worry and wonder about each other. During his long ordeal, Joseph was still upset but he knew I loved him and would never betray his trust. He remained puzzled, but instead of ventilating his hurt feelings, he waited in patient faith and went to sleep on it.

And so did I . . . And you see how well it all worked out?

### Prayer to Mary

Bless me, Mary, with your words and attitude. And ask your husband to teach me how to get over my hurts. And even when I'm upset, bless me with a good night's sleep before I act out of anger.

You know, sometimes I am weighed down because of the selfish or hostile behavior of others. Still lodged in my heart and head is evidence of my being mistreated in some way: rejection, scorn, manipulation.

*(Here, think of people who have wronged you. Take the "witness stand" and speak of the details in your case as Fact 1, Fact 2, etc., as Joseph might have done against Mary if anger or retaliation controlled him.)*

Mary, you see how my thoughts go sour sometimes, don't you? Take all this court trial stuff from my heart. Lead me to Joseph. Let's the three of us sit around a table, or by a quiet porch someplace. Then teach me how to be more patient with people and more creative about possibilities that might come out of a bad scene. Let me be less judgmental and more patient.

Please, Mary, much more patient. Amen.

### *Prayer for Others*

Blessed Mary, take my personal prayer and let it be my prayer for others. I speak now of certain ones I know who are hurting very much because of how other people are mistreating them or leaving them uncared for:

1. Some suffer from abuse, bad temper, and the silent treatment by members of their own family.

2. Some suffer from the callousness of those they work with, or those they work for, or those who work under them. *(Mention the particulars.)*

3. Some suffer from rejection by their friends. It may be that they have been hurt by a rebuke of some kind, or confused by another's behavior in the same way as Joseph was.

4. It could be any of these hurts, or something else. *(Tell Mary the details, as much as you know of the story.)*

Please, Mary, help them to get out of the rut of sadness they're in. The loss of one friend, the disruptive antics of one person in the family, or on the job—this doesn't mean their whole life is blown apart.

Let good friends nourish them with loyal love. Let quiet prayer restore balance to their lives. And especially, give them the grace of your example. Lead them to a quiet room and then to a comfortable chair. Let Joseph talk to them about trust in God and trust in you, Mary. Let his good working hands rub the tenseness out of their shoulders, wipe the tears from their eyes, and remind them how good things so often happen when they handle their hurts quietly and go to sleep on it. Amen.

# *The Nativity*

[Near Bethlehem] Mary brought forth her son and wrapped him in soft clothes and laid him in a manger. . . . And the shepherds and all who witnessed these events marveled. . . . But Mary kept them in mind, pondering them over in her heart.                                        Luke 2:1–19

### *Mary Speaks to You*
On that first Christmas, I was filled with mixed emotions. The mood Joseph and I shared had many more dimensions than what artwork and Christmas cards imply. Those representations have me either bursting with happiness or serenely composed in an attitude of wonder. But there was more than this. When it came to confidence in God and faith in God's love-project, I was filled with gratitude and awe. As angels and onlookers praised me for what was so obviously the beginning of wondrous deeds, I was humbly proud of my part in the divine developments.

More than any other proof of God's presence, the birth of Jesus was the most joyful; so there were good feelings, of course. But there was another side too. I was prayerfully cautious about trying to understand God's plan. I didn't want to do it too quickly. There was a certain anxiety veiling the events—a shiver of foreboding doom. Oh, there was no doubt in my mind about God's part in what would happen. The doubts concerned the *human* element. I knew the Scriptures well—all about the heroes and heroines, the sages and prophets, how they spoke genuinely about God's will and, because of it, were usually rejected and even martyred. The angels proclaimed that Jesus would be God's hero, spokesman, and sage; so he would suffer too. This was the prophetic shadow that dimmed my joy.

Another human drawback was my own anxiety. As I said, I did have confidence and faith in God, but I wondered how I would manage. Does that surprise you? Do you think I had such self-assurance that I could step right into my role as Mother of God without a qualm? Not so. It's difficult for any mother to bring up her baby. And this baby was so special. I wondered: How do I teach the Word of God to speak words? Dare I call Jesus and tell him to come home for supper? How do I tell Divinity to eat his vegetables because they are good for him? How would I manage, how would it all work out?

These and many more worries were swirling around as I cuddled my baby and proudly showed him to the shepherds. As I say, this was a time of joy to outmatch any other. It was also a time of wonder and concern over the awesome challenge I had to face . . . and live with. I was told to continue as well as I could, with just the experience and equipment I had.

You know how heady the future can be. Isn't it sometimes that way for you? You are happy to be alive, grateful for the gifts God has given you and opportunities that have come your way. Yet, at the same time, you feel like me—anxious about what you'll do in such and such a circumstance, wondering if things will work out, and what to do if they don't work out.

Talk to me. Let me be a part of your real world, especially during those times when you experience joy that carries worry with it. I'll comfort you and support you. I know how. I've been down the road of mixed emotions, and I want to help you down that road as well.

### *Prayer to Mary*

Thank you, Blessed Mary, for your understanding. I feel better knowing I can talk to you about the pluses and minuses in my life that seem so tangled.

Some parts of my life I really enjoy. Let me tell you about a few of them:

*(Here, talk about some things you find challenging and joy-inducing, things you either enjoy by yourself or that are related to family, friends, location, job, hobbies, etc., or whatever you want to mention at this time of prayer.)*

These are wonderful things; I could almost call them Christmassy. They are the pluses in my existence, Mary. But mixed in with the goodness and my gratefulness are doubts about the future. Self-doubts too: How long can I continue with *(name the person or persons)*, or in the situation of *(describe it)*? What will happen when *(name the person)* grows up? When I *(or we)* grow old? How will I adjust if *(describe the situation)* takes place, or doesn't turn out, or turns out wrong?

Please understand me, Mary. I'm not griping. I'm not ruining my world with worries. I try to do what I can with the confusion in my life. That's why I thank you for telling me how your Christmas really was—with all the apprehension and joy you felt. I'll continue to do what I can, with the competence I have, the friends I can count on, and the God I trust in.

You did. And it all worked out for you. So thank you, my Lady, and, once again, *Mary* Christmas! Amen.

### *Pray for Others*

And now, Blessed Mother, look with love on those I have concern for. They, too, struggle with self-doubts. Some days they find it difficult to put one foot into the future. They are ground down by their sense of unworthiness or bitterness. Dismal aspects of life so permeate their minds that they cannot always be open to the possibilities of joy. Even God's love seems unsubstantial.

*(Here, mention those who are unhappy because of hurt feelings, anxieties about the future, or because their lives are uprooted or made bankrupt or torn apart because of family problems, unemployment, hatred, or grief. In your own words, ask Mary to bring these people to the Sacred Heart of her son. Pray silently for as long as it seems right to you. Conclude with these words:)*

Please reach them with your understanding, Mary. Help them to pick up their lives with courage and self-confidence. Lead them to your son, Jesus. He makes everlasting Christmas possible for all of us.

Give them this hope, Mary. Share with them your joy. Let them find comfort in your Christmas story and in the Wonderful Son who came from both God and you. Amen.

# The Presentation

When the time came to present Jesus to the Lord, Mary and Joseph went to Jerusalem. . . . There was a man named Simeon. . . . He took the child in his arms and blessed God. . . . Then he said to Mary, "This child is destined for the rise and fall of many . . . and a sword shall pierce your heart." Anna was also there. She, too, gave praise to God and spoke to all who would listen.                    Luke 2:22–40

## Mary Speaks to You

Of course, you realize I was not under strict obligation to present my child in the Temple forty days after his birth. This was the duty of other parents in Israel: to obey a law that recognized that God was the source of all life. In a lovely ritual that expressed gratitude to God, parents offered their gift of new life—their child—to the Creator. Then they would buy the child back and offer God a "replacement gift": a pair of turtle doves. It is a good law, a noble custom embracing a beautiful prayer.

But, as I mentioned, Joseph and I didn't have to do this. Our child was already consecrated to God the moment he was conceived in my womb. The God-man, Emmanuel, was instantly commissioned to be the perfect return of gratitude for the gift of life. Even so, we were glad to fulfill the legal requirements. The idea that motivated Joseph and me was not "It's something we've got to do, so we might as well get it over with!" What urged us to make the long trip from Nazareth to Jerusalem was the idea that here was a wonderful opportunity to thank God for our baby . . . and for the plan of love that God began . . . and for the joy that Jesus would bring into the world.

Then came the blessings. An old man and an old woman

were given hope and consolation because of what we did that day. Simeon was very old, worn out, and close to death. But a certain instinct promised him the good news that he would not meet death until he saw the Messiah, the Chosen One. We brought that good news with us. Now he could finally relax, close his eyes, and smile at the prospect of eternal happiness with the God of his search, now the God of his comfort.

Then Anna came on the scene. She was not feeble. She was one of the wisest persons I ever met. She was quite old, too, but age didn't take away her zest for life; it made her more serene, wiser. We had a marvelous afternoon together, Anna, Joseph, and I. And we always stayed with her, for the next eleven years of her life, whenever we went to Jerusalem.

That is the blessing I was talking about. Because we did more than we had to do, in regard to the Law—and went out of our way to show gratitude to God—we were able to be the instrument of consolation for one old man who was about to die. And we developed a wonderful friendship with a woman who was more wise than feeble, more strong than sick, and one of the most unforgettable persons I ever met. She gave more to us than we ever gave to her.

I'm sure you have friends like this yourself. I pray that you do. I also pray that you reconsider laws (and everything that you have to do) with creativity and optimism, looking for what unforeseen surprises might arise from duty done without complaining.

### Prayer to Mary

Bless me, Mary. Help me to be less sensitive about my own rights: what other people owe me or what I don't have to do because it's not my job or not my turn. Stop my quick impulses to complain: "It's not fair that so and so depends on me so much," or "It's about time other people pulled some of the load in this or that area."

*(Here, express your complaints to Mary: how you feel that other people are using you, or neglecting you, or taking you for granted, or not honoring their responsibilities. Tell Mary about these things, in your own words.)*

You see, Mary, I do have the right to grumble about other people's laziness or lack of consideration. And I have the right, strictly speaking, to pull back and do only the bare minimum. But you had the right not to go the Temple. According to the strict interpretation of the Law, you didn't have to make that pilgrimage to Jerusalem. But if you had decided not to go, you wouldn't have been able to use such a gracious opportunity to thank God, or have been able to console an ailing man or be consoled by a new friend. You were impelled by much more noble motives than doing only as much as you had to. And see how well it worked out?

Mary, give me eyes like yours. Help me to look for similar opportunities. Don't allow me to start counting the cost, or considering it a chore when I care for the elderly or visit the sick. Often, what I do for them will give them peace to their last days, as you did for Simeon. Also, there may be a blessing for me when I give my time to anyone in need. Anna became a big plus in your life, Mary. Those I care for can become a big plus in my life too. Some already have.

*(Here, mention some friends who became your friends in much the same way that Mary and Anna developed their friendship. You were "doing your duty" somewhere, or "volunteering for a cause" in some way, and you happened to meet, and the friend-*

*ship developed. Tell Mary about some of the details. It will be good for both of you to hear these stories.)*

Love finds many different ways to grow. Friendships start under surprising circumstances. Good friends are already the most precious part of my life. Please help me, Mary, so that I can be even more grateful for them. Amen.

### *Prayer for Others*

First, Blessed Mary, I pray for all the Simeons and Annas in my life. Be with them in a special way. I am so grateful for their love and friendship. Please be their special friend as well.

I also pray for people who are old or dependent on others in any way. The sick and the aging can get cantankerous sometimes. Impatience and despondency are easy attitudes for them to slip into. Give them the consolation you gave Simeon. Let Jesus come with you to close their eyes in peace when it is time.

Finally, Mary, bless all the people who care for the sick and the elderly.

*(Here, mention the ones you know personally. Let your prayer be as detailed as seems right. Then pray for all those who are in any way connected with the healing and helping professions.)*

They are good people, all of them. But sometimes they get frustrated. It's difficult to be always patient, always on call, always cheerful. Sometimes they are cross or impatient in their mannerisms; sometimes they distance themselves or speak harsh words to those they care for.

Smooth out their ruffled conduct, Mary. Ease the aches of their frustrations. Let them be with the ones they nurse as you were with Simeon and Anna. There will be a blessing in it, if they do.

I know you will help them. Please inspire us to have Christ's Spirit in all the ways that we give—and are given—consolation. Amen.

# *Jesus in the Temple*

When Jesus was twelve years old, they went up to Jerusalem . . . and when they started their journey back, Jesus remained in the city. They searched for him . . . and after three days, they found him in the Temple, listening to the teachers and asking them questions. Mary and Joseph were astonished. And his mother said to him, "Son, why have you acted this way to us? In torment, your father and I have been looking for you." Jesus said, "Why did you do that? Did you not know that I must be in my Father's house, concerned with my Father's affairs?" They did not understand . . . And his mother kept all these things carefully in her heart.                                           Luke 2:41–52

### *Mary Speaks to You*
Notice how the last joyful mystery is right before the sorrowful mysteries. That unforgettable day when I found my twelve-year-old son in the Temple, my joy in finding him was only momentary, but the anguish that came as a result of what happened was a much more lasting emotion. I'm talking about the sadness that came after the event; not the terror Joseph and I had while we were searching for him frantically. Losing a child in any city is bad enough; but to lose Jesus when Jerusalem was teeming with people on pilgrimage—you can imagine our panic and anxiety!

When we found him, joy made us forget our anguish—

for a moment. Then came the blow that permanently changed my outlook on life, and my style of prayer as well.

Jesus had taken initiative for the first time in his life. After all, by our law, he was entitled to. He was twelve years old, the age of *bar mitzvah,* the age that our social custom considers the time when someone becomes subject to the Law. So what he did was not as the child Jesus, but the responsible adult Jesus. Just the same, it never occurred to Joseph or me that he would take on his responsibilities so soon, and so seriously!

Joseph was hurt even more than I was. I had blurted out, "Your father and I had our insides all torn up searching for you!" Then I noticed how strangely solemn my son looked. He did not reply the way I expected. He didn't apologize, or explain his behavior, or agree that we must have felt terrible anguish. Nothing like that. Our son seemed to be distant to us—the focus of his world was not with us. He was dignified in his bearing, in a way he never was before, thoughtful beyond his years, heavy with profound purpose. It seemed as though he had just made a pact with death and joined himself with all the tragic prophets of our history.

"Why did you seek me?" was his strange reply. If such words were said by another child, in less mysterious circumstances, it would have been effrontery. Indeed, why shouldn't we be searching for him? Why shouldn't we be worried? He was lost in a big city, and we had searched for days.

Of course, his words were not insulting, but they were puzzling. He spoke as he did because he was filled with the details of his own destiny. He could not think of anything else. I felt sorry for Joseph when Jesus then said, "I am occupied fully in my Father's affairs!" He meant, of course, his Father God. The man he usually called father was left out of consideration. This, too, was part of his high seriousness that overshadowed everything else. Even so, I could tell that my husband was hurt, sidelined. The only thing that was real to Jesus was the task of love he was prepared to take up.

When some of this fuller meaning dawned on us, Joseph and I were different people. We were changed, all three of us. Joseph was reminded of his role as foster father. Jesus, in a mature way, accepted his commission to be the Great Prophet of Israel. And I was changed in my role also. Instead of being an ordinary mother of an ordinary family of Nazareth, I was reminded that I must be a most extraordinary mother of a most amazing son, who would be a sword of contradiction for all peoples and, in the course of time, would pierce his own mother's heart with sorrow.

I wanted to put all this in its natural setting, telling you the way it really was and the way it really felt—so that I can help you understand how I appreciate your turmoil when you face changes in life, or when you experience anxiety, or when someone shocks you by what they do or say to you . . . or when they, like Jesus, decide things on their own without informing or consulting you.

I appreciate how you feel when such things happen in your life. They happened in my life too. I know how to console you. And I want to.

### *Prayer to Mary*

Blessed Mary, I didn't realize you went through anxieties so similar to mine. Jesus and you already know what I'm going through. Even so, it is healing for me to mention it in prayer.

*(Here, tell Mary in your own words about the changes and challenges in your life: getting older, facing retirement, hearing a*

*diagnosis of cancer, preparing to graduate from school, facing mature responsibilities for the first time, planning to move to a new town or job, facing new challenges of a growing family, knowing you must act on a crisis at work, being forced to do something about a compulsion, being forced into a financial crunch, or something else. Talk about these things with Mary, as you would to a friend.)*

Mary, help me to know what is the right thing to do and the right time to do it. Ask Jesus to help me prepare for the future as well as I can, to help me to continue, no matter how my decisions turn out.

You didn't know how you would manage once your son reached his teenage years. You knew there would be sadness and great hardships ahead, but whatever might come up, you were ready to do the best you could.

Help me, Mary, to develop the serenity you had. Let me keep growing, no matter how the ups and downs of life may greet me. In the mix of your joys and sorrows, confidence and anxieties, you treasured all that happened to you. You treasured God's mysteries of love, and so must I: pondering them over and over in my heart. Amen.

### Prayer for Others

Mary, let me return to the list I already mentioned and let me focus my prayer on behalf of those I love. There is a litany of concerns for the people I work with, shop with, have lunch with, and sometimes meet by chance. Each of them has cares and fears for the future and wonders how he or she will manage.

Your heart is large, Mary. You and Joseph know what it means to change directions in life. Be with my friends and encourage them to face their encounters well.

Take them to your son, who will never leave them without direction or strength. And make sure, no matter how troublesome God's way may seem at the time, that they always treasure the love they have been given. Help them to grow in the kind of prayer that ponders God's mysterious ways and to live in the certain knowledge of God's love. Amen.

# Sorrowful Mysteries

# The Agony in the Garden

When Jesus came to Gethsemane he began to be disturbed and troubled. And he said, "My soul is very sorrowful—even to death." Then he fell on the ground and prayed that, if it was possible, this agony might pass. And his sweat became like drops of blood. Then, when he rose from prayer, he went to his disciples and found them sleeping, for their eyes were heavy.

Mark 14:36–42; Matthew 26:39–46; Luke 22:42–46

## Mary Speaks to You

As you know, I wasn't there, that last night of my son's ordeal. No one was there really—no one to give him support. No one is ever there when we go through the agony of alienation. It is a terrible feeling, that all-aloneness, when we fall suddenly into the pit of utter abandonment!

We can talk about such occasions, but they can never really be shared, never satisfactorily explained.

My son learned this the hard way. Don't we all? He appealed to his apostles to grit it out with him, to support him as the prospect of Good Friday's cruelty caught up to his consciousness in full force. "Stay with me," he pleaded. "I need to have the feeling that some people are with me now. Human hatred, spawned by envy and greed, is almost too much for me to bear! Let me see that what I'm doing is a good and noble thing to do. Please!"

No. It didn't happen. No one supported Jesus. He had to face the horror all by himself. It did help, he told me afterward, to know that I was with him in spirit and that we were worth saving by his redemptive act. Thinking about this helped, but he still sweated profusely, as though he was bleeding. I don't think there is any sorrow more poignant than being alienated from people we have loved or knowing that the life we have lived will soon be cast aside.

I felt something of that sorrow when Jesus left Nazareth and began his active ministry. Oh, he would come back, now and then, for a visit. But his new home was Capernaum, by the Sea of Galilee. From there he gathered disciples and started to heal and preach.

Of course, this meant that my house suddenly became a tomb. Thirty years is a long time to get used to one way of life. I'd sing while I did my work. I'd look out at the hills and fields I knew so well. I was so happy. There was a rhythm to our years: day followed day, feast followed feast—the ordinary life with its blessings.

Then everything changed. My son's room was so bare, so unlived in, I didn't want to look at it. The news I received—about what he was doing and where he was—came to me in bits and pieces, and mostly garbled. Seldom was it any more than rumors, gossip, hearsay stuff. Even so, I did hear wonderful reports on how people rushed to him for healing and how they marveled at his words. Then, with ever-increasing alarm, came bad news about his standoffs with the Pharisees and his diminished popularity because people (so many of them) were reluctant to change their lives.

These troubling reports increased my sorrow. Now I felt doubly alienated. I was separated from my son and I was powerless to help him. Oh, sometimes I joined the disciples as they followed the Lord. It was good just to be near him, but it wasn't the same as it used to be. The good old days at Nazareth never did come back.

You know how it is. If you don't really comprehend how Jesus felt in his agony, at least you can appreciate how I felt when I was left alone. At any rate, you surely know how you feel when that happens to you.

I know what you're going through. I will be with you at those times. Don't lose heart. Turn to me and to my son. We are here for you.

### Prayer to Mary

Mary, my mother, be that same presence for me as you were for Jesus. You weren't physically present when Jesus suffered his agony in the garden, but he knew you were close to him. You aren't physically present to me, either, but I know you are here.

It isn't easy feeling left out. I think of happier, livelier times before. I think of other people enjoying themselves with a caring family and understanding friends; and here am I, outside of things, feeling like an outcast, just as you were, Mary, when Jesus left home.

I'm sometimes very much afraid of what will follow after the loneliness really sets in. I'm getting older. Death has claimed many loved ones already, and worse than death is the sadness I feel when friends I used to have are now too busy, or too distant, or too infirm to be friends any more. We have lost interest in one another and in what we used to share.

These things happen. I'm not judging anyone, Mary. I just wish, as you did, for simpler, happier, full-with-friendship times that used to be, and aren't any more.

Be with me in these sorrows, Mary. Anchor me so that I don't wander away. I know you are with me just as much as you were with Jesus. It helps me simply to spell out my fears and ask your help with words that express my deepest longings. Amen.

### Prayer for Others

I think of those, Mary, who are going through their own version of the agony in the garden:

*(Here, mention the people you know who are hurting because their children have grown up and left the nest; or their friends at work have been laid off and their job is not the same; or their spouse died; or their friends have left them or aren't very friendly anymore; or they must leave the neighborhood or the job and start fresh somewhere else; or, as in the case of Jesus, influential people who control popular opinion, are determined to hurt them. Mention whatever else is causing their sense of alienation.)*

Please be with them, Blessed Mary. Comfort their hearts with your presence. Don't let them turn sour on life. They need some way to weather their time of sorrow. Jesus found his way, by letting God's will of love be done, even in his agony. That must be their way, also. When sorrows are joined to prayer, and prayer is linked to your prayer for them, they can carry on, no matter what. Even agony can be accepted in God's name.

Help them to understand this mystery, my Lady. Help them to see how real love sometimes is revealed in deepest sorrow. Amen.

# *The Scourging*

When Pilate saw that he was gaining nothing, but rather that a riot was beginning, he released the man who was in prison for murder and had Jesus scourged . . . and then delivered him over to be crucified.

Mark 15:12–15; Matthew 27:22–26; Luke 23:21–25

## *Mary Speaks to You*

The mystery of my son's scourging is shrouded behind prison walls. After the Resurrection, some of the disciples told me of a few of the details of that horrible scene. Jesus didn't spell it out. Jesus referred to it only as his "birth pangs that brought life" (see John 16:20–22).

Later on, the early church glossed over what might be considered television news today, such as, how many strokes there were, how much blood was spilled, how many soldiers did it, how violent the look of cruelty was in their faces, things like that.

What matters is not so much what was done, but why. The torture at the scourging post was God's way of telling us that no human can escape physical pain and the feeling of helplessness when the process of death begins. The scourging also tells us that the pre-death indignities the body endures should never be considered the end of anyone's life. Easter's victory over such indignities is what ushers in eternal life.

I followed Jesus' lead and remained silent about my own pains as I was preparing to die many years later. Of course, I suffered from the lack of freedom that came with growing old. I felt bad about it; it frightened me as I sank down, little by little, into a strange sense of tiredness. I suffered no great afflictions as I grew old. And I was not crushed by any abrupt violence as my son was. There were no whips on my back, no sense of loss because life was cut short at a young age. Not those things.

Chances are that you won't suffer like Jesus, either. But you will feel pain, and the loss and confusion that comes with any serious sickness or breakdown of the body's functions. You know these things will come to you, if they haven't already.

You know something about why my son suffered— inside himself—as cruel blows were carving out his flesh. But along with knowing that, you should also realize how he wanted to give meaning to the fears endured by every patient in every hospital and by every victim of all the scourging posts and in all the Auschwitzes of the world. You see, Jesus took upon himself the suffering of us all, the woes of everyone who has ever been afraid of death or treated cruelly in any way. My son was vividly aware of the suffering of all humanity as he became the victim of the sins of all humanity.

### Prayer to Mary

Thank you, Mary, for telling me about this mystery. You've given me a clue to understanding the mystery of evil. It used to be so difficult to meditate on our Lord's scourging. I couldn't even imagine anyone suffering so much. It was hard to meditate on the horrible things that happened to our Lord on Good Friday morning.

Now you let me see how I can join Jesus in his suffering and how I can let him link me closer to his redemptive love. Some shocks in life I have already experienced:

*(Here, mention the accidents and other emergencies you have had, or whatever circumstances in your life that required medical attention. Mention perhaps the physical setbacks you have experienced as you have grown older. Also bring up how you have suffered as you cared for others.)*

Blessed Mary, these things have been real concerns in my life. Pain and the fear of death are part of everyone's life. As situations like these come up or continue, take me by the hand and stay very close to me. Remind me that pain is not all there is, that suffering and loss are not the end of everything. Life and love come after the sorrow. So it was with Jesus. He proved life's dignity by his patient acceptance of indignity. Love's staying power showed itself at the scourging post and along the way to the cross. Life's energy lasted long after sins had any more power to crush him.

Give me the staying power Jesus had. Mary, let me remember you and your son whenever pain prompts me to push the panic button, whenever I think about the end of my life. And let me prove faithful in the same way all great lovers do—by seeing the meaning in my suffering when it is joined to honest love. Amen.

### *Prayer for Others*
Now, Mary, I ask you to turn your attention to:

*(Here, mention the names and particulars of those who have undergone surgery; or who have had tragic accidents; or who are pathetically handicapped or senile; or who are victims of wars, AIDS, poverty, dispossession, vendettas, or vindictiveness. Tell Mary in your own words how much you feel for them.)*

Mary, do for them what you have already done for me. Take them by the hand and lead them inside the heart of your son. Together, let you and them go past his bleeding flesh and feeble frame and all the scars of human cruelty— past all of this, and let them dwell inside the God-man who put up with it for the sake of love.

May those I pray for, Mary, be more patient in their suffering and come alive to the confidence of Christ and his power to help them wait for Easter. Amen.

# *The Crowning with Thorns*

The soldiers led him inside the palace and they clothed him in a purple cloak and put on him a crown of thorns. And kneeling before him, they mocked him: "Hail, King of the Jews."                    Matthew 27:27–31; Mark 15:16–20

## *Mary Speaks to You*

Jesus told me, after Easter, that the crowning with thorns was the worst sorrow of them all. The other monstrosities were events that showed wickedness for what it was. None of it was easy to endure. But this one was different. When the squad of mercenaries crowned Jesus with thorns, they made fun of the very things that he was. It wasn't just character assassination; it was character ridicule!

The Son of God was born of me and grew up slowly; and when the time was right, he preached and healed and trained his disciples with a set of purposes that were all bound up with love and service of others. As Messiah, he was the fulfillment of Jewish hopes; as king, he was the satisfaction of everyone's longing; as suffering servant, he was the comfort of all who sorrow; as the crucified one, he was the pardon of all sins; as resurrected one, he was the promise of everlasting life.

All of this was, and still is, the glory of my son. And yet the soldiers scorned the qualities that were the very best in him: virtue, kindness, compassion for all, wisdom, a teaching skill that reached all people, freedom from fear, forgiveness of sins, absolute sovereignty of a kingdom of peace and health and graciousness. These magnificent qualities were ridiculed mercilessly.

It seemed as if the whole world shouted down the marvelous gifts that God wanted to give the world. It was as if God were saying: "Here you are. Here is my son, with all his attributes and charm." Yet humans—so many humans—were shoving it all away in contempt: "We don't want your gifts, God, and we don't want the giver!" Not only was Jesus rejected, but he was sneered at, simply for trying to rescue them.

Jesus was powerless to defend himself. What more could he do? Or say? He had already done it all, said it all. Now everything he stood for was treated with contempt.

I felt something of his passion, three years earlier. When my son left home, I was stuck with bad-tempered neighbors who treated me so uncivilly. Jesus had claimed, in their synagogue, that he was the promised Messiah, that all they had hoped for would come true through him. His townsfolk were so enraged at what he said that they wanted to seize him and hurl him headlong over a cliff. But Jesus would not be intimidated; he walked right through that ring of bullies. Then he packed his bag and left home for good, setting up his base of ministry in the Capernaum area.

*He* left home, and it was over with. But I was left to go through day-to-day life with those sullen, grudge-keeping villagers. You know how small minds work when a hero shows them up and walks away. They take out their frustrations on his family. That's what they did to me. They scorned me when I went to the market. They excluded me from the town's activities. They whispered to one another about my pretense of being the mother of the Messiah. They treated me with contempt—the most hurtful kind was the contempt of silence. I suffered in much the same way Jesus did when he was given over to the cruelty of the palace guards.

I tell you this so that you might know how both of us have experienced the hurts that come from derision and contempt. We know, Jesus and I. We have both been viciously treated. And so we understand what's going on with you when you endure suffering similar to ours. We understand, and we can help.

### Prayer to Mary

Blessed Mary, as soon as you put yourself into the picture, I sense the meaning of this mystery a little better. Because of your sorrow, I have a more tender feeling for the terrible atrocity inflicted on your son.

Of course, I have never been asked to undergo the ridicule he endured. My kind of sorrow has been closer to yours, my Lady. I have felt the sting of gossips. I've been snubbed and ridiculed for qualities I prize most dearly.

I tried to impress people, win them over to my way of thinking, or simply live at peace with them. I couldn't do it. All I could do was feel their scorn. When people dismiss a person's best qualities and treat them with disdain, that's the most poignant sorrow of all.

I need you, Mary, when I endure my version of your snubbing at Nazareth, my version of your son's crowning with thorns. You knew Jesus appreciated you for who you were and this helped you to bear it all. Jesus was able to continue in his trials because he knew of your love, that you would never turn your back on him or mock the person he was.

Each of you helped the other by giving dignity and respect to the one you loved. Mary, I need you both to be with me in the same way. When bitter or grudge-filled individuals try to put me down or make fun of me, I need you and your son to remind me of my worth. Give me the grace to pick myself up when I am down; and most of all, Mary, remind me how much value I have in the eyes of God and all God's friends. Amen.

### Prayer for Others

Now I pray on behalf of those from every tribe, city, nation, and ethnic group. I pray for all those who are made fun of for being what they are:

*(Here, mention the silent ones, muzzled in POW or refugee camps, convicts imprisoned without fair trial, and those chained to themselves by their own obsessive behavior. Mention also individuals who have been excluded from an organization they wanted to belong to, children who are teased by other children, those who are taunted by jokes, by bigots and gossips. Also include those who suffer from a family member's scorn of silence, or from the angry behavior of other family members. Mention other individuals or groups as they come to you. Speak of them in your own words.)*

Indeed, Mary, I pray for all who undergo heartaches similar to what you suffered when you were left alone among the sour-faced villagers of Nazareth. Since my friends at times are like you in their sorrows, stand by them the way you stayed faithful to Jesus. Let them appreciate their dignity and the promise of blessings they will receive at their own Easter when God will wipe away their tears, and the blessedness of paradise will open them up to a world of gratitude, a world protected from the arrows of all scorn. Amen.

# *Jesus Carries His Cross*

After they had mocked him, they stripped him of the purple robe, and put his own clothes on him, and led him away to crucify him. . . . And there followed him a great multitude of people, and of women who bewailed and lamented him.
Luke 23:26–32; Matthew 27:31; Mark 15:20

## *Mary Speaks to You*
Because everyone has suffered from a sense of helpless-

ness, this sorrowful mystery is the easiest one to identify with. Even so, it is so painful to talk about it. I suppose that's the experience of most people. You can describe cruelty or thoughtlessness in detail. There is something palpable, as well as painful, when forceful whips tear apart the skin or when derisive words and gestures mock the soul. But how can you comment on helplessness? That's a feeling that is just there. You can't do a thing about it.

I tell you this so that I can be confident that you understand how I felt as I stood by helplessly when Jesus, with the cross on his shoulder, passed me by. I was there along his route to Golgotha, the Hill of the Skull. I witnessed it all—when Jesus was sentenced, when he started out with his burden and stumbled through the narrow streets. We met halfway to Golgotha. Our eyes locked in sorrow. But what could he say to me? What could I say to him?

Nothing. That is exactly what transpired—nothing! Imagine a mother telling her son to cheer up under such conditions. Or imagine asking "How are you?" Or anything. Even to wish he would speak my name would be a burden for him, he was so weak. I just stood by on the sidelines of his suffering, and he passed on.

Jesus was as helpless for me as I was for him. All both of us could do, that afternoon, was to endure the throbbing dullness of it all—the absolute inability to comfort ourselves or each other. Our faithful endurance would serve as a model of stability for all people. Everyone will be able to find comfort when the time comes to endure the suffering I call "the sadness of the helpless bystander."

That is precisely what we were, my Son and I—mute spectators of the other's sorrowful heart. We were both victims of the anger and envy of others. We were made impotent by their sins. I want you to grasp—deep down inside you—the "bystander sorrow" that afflicted me, because I want you to trust me when I speak of my wanting to comfort you. I have a kindred feeling for your grief, especially when it has to do with feeling helpless. Jesus and I are with you as you stand by while other people (friends, family, associates in whatever circumstances) are suffering. You'd very much like to be an angel of mercy, an instrument of healing, but all you are is you, and all you can do is just be there.

I want you to know that Jesus and I will be there too.

### *Prayer to Mary*

Thank you, Mary, for understanding. It's hard to put into words the frustration and sadness that accompany my helplessness. But it's good to realize that you know all about it. You have grieved in the same way I am grieving now. Help me to be a good presence for the people that I love:

*(Here, mention the members of your family, friends, and fellow workers who are suffering from circumstances outside their control: wives who are mistreated by their husbands, or vice versa; children who are terrorized by parents or by a gang; employees or employers who are manipulated; colleagues who are victims of character assassination; people who suffer the effects of poverty, natural calamity, harassment, or injustice. Also, pray for those who are hurting from pressures within: bitterness of soul, cynicism, despair, alcoholism, drug addiction, or other kinds of compulsion.)*

Please, Mary, notice all these people on my list, and add to them the ones I have forgotten. I want so much to help them, but I can't. No one can, not for a while anyway. They must carry their own cross, by themselves, until they hit bottom and want to change; or a "good break" lifts them up from the hole they are in; or time eases their bitterness of spirit; or love finds a way to change their angry or evil disposition.

Be with me, Mary, as I grieve with them. And when my frustration tends to become bitter and my sorrow edges close to despair, take my hand and tell me how you've been there too; and now you are here, with me. Amen.

### Prayer for Others

Blessed Mary, look again at the list I just made. Before I was praying for *my* helplessness as I attended the sorrows of others. Now I pray for all those who must stand by helplessly, as loved ones in their lives are feeling pain.

Too often, when people are forced into the role of impotent bystander, they flex their anger-muscles against God for letting it happen, or they start taking out their frustrations on others. They sometimes lose control and beat up on others or themselves because they simply can't do anything about a situation.

Take their hand, too, Mary. Be a comfort to them whenever impatience nags them to do something, when in fact there is nothing they can do. Help them to realize that often the only option is simply to stand beside someone on their way of the cross.

Help them to wait for the time of Christ's ultimate promise, when human injustices will cease forever, at the end of time. Then all creation will witness the end of cruelties and indignities, and there will be no more oppression, or tears, or standing by helplessly. Then it will be all right.

But my friends and I have to have some comfort as we wait for that time. Be this comfort, blessed Mary. Look upon those I pray for and give them hope in their present pain. Give hope to us all. Amen.

# *The Crucifixion*

There stood by the cross of Jesus: his mother, his mother's sister, Mary of Cleopas and Mary Magdalene and [John] the disciple whom Jesus loved. . . .

Then Jesus said, "It is finished!" And, having bowed his head, he gave up his spirit.                John 19:25–30

Jesus cried out with a loud voice: "Father, into your hands I commend my spirit!" And having said this, he breathed his last.                                                    Luke 23:46

Jesus cried out with a loud voice and yielded up his spirit.
                                                            Matthew 27:50

Jesus uttered a loud cry and breathed his last.    Mark 15:37

## *Mary Speaks to You*

During the three hours on the cross, time just waited for the last cry death would utter. Then, for the next thirty-seven hours or so, until Easter dawn, all we could think about in the upper room was death's apparent victory.

Death. Death. Death. Everything Christ stood for—the significance of his teachings, the purpose of his healings—*everything* rose or fell, depending on who would win the ultimate contest: the devil and death, or Jesus and life. Jesus had a wonderful way with words; he had a knack for directing the mind toward considerations that were both prayerful and profound. His teachings, mostly, prepared us for the next life, assuring us that he had the power to give us the joys of his eternal life. They pointedly asserted that the very purpose for his coming into our world was to give us clear passage to unending life.

Then he gave up his spirit. The flesh of the Word-made-flesh no longer functioned. Jesus had to experience the end of what would be the end of everything if it were not for the power of the Resurrection.

From the time my son was twelve years old, he was fascinated by death. What does it mean for a human to end up with nothing, going nowhere? Is that all there is? Can death mock life so casually? He was very angry at the deaths of Joseph and of Lazarus his friend, and he agonized about the prospect of what it would be like for him when he would breathe no more.

All people think a lot about this mystery, whether they admit it or not. Some try to distance themselves from the problem and not talk about it. Some choose excitement to distract them for a few years from the inevitable; some dabble in superstitions that they hope will control death's finality; others insist on being too busy to bother with such morbid thoughts.

But it's still there. Death does not go away. Always, the omen of destruction looms.

I have heard the cries and the prayers from my sons and daughters for all generations. How unfair it is that anyone should die! That's right, it's not fair! If humans can perform such deeds of heroism, fall in love so tenderly, radiate their humanness with such music, art, and stories that make their world so wonderful, how can they end up as nothing? God created us for *life*. There must be an eternal "place" where we can continue to manifest and express our gifts: loveliness, artistry, and wisdom.

Such are the best of human thoughts, the most telling of

all human hopes. Such was the wish-fulfillment of my son. Notice, I didn't say just "wish"; I also said "fulfillment."

We need to be confident in the life God has given us. We need to know it will last forever. So Jesus cried out with a loud voice and carried all our fears of death with him. Then he waited, as I and the disciples waited, for Easter to anchor our hopes and honor the pledge of all God's promises.

My son's greatest sermon was the wordless cry from the cross. His greatest heroism was that apparent defeat. His most significant victory took place when it seemed that his enemies had vanquished him. Love made its most telling message when he screamed in pain, gave up his spirit, and finally died.

We died with him that day. The *awe-full-ness* of what he went through has brought consolation to us all. I am alive, here in heaven, thanks to Jesus' death. You have the same happiness to look forward to. You do. You really do! Death has been defeated forever. Jesus has made life timeless, ushered in by love.

Be assured of this love, this life. The only ultimate truth worth trusting is the life and death, and then the life again, of Jesus.

When you give your body over to death, do it in remembrance of Jesus. And remember also all the promises he made about seeing you again, where your joy will be full, and nothing will ever tamper with your happiness.

### *Prayer to Mary*

Blessed Mary, I don't pretend to understand the deepest things that are part of me. I don't understand why I was born, or why I grew up during this time of history or in the family I was placed in, and with the talents and the intelligence I have. I don't know where my noblest thoughts come from, or

gentlest loves, or under what lucky circumstances the happiest times seem to have come into my life and thrilled me.

And I don't know why those people and things I've been
most attracted to must die. Why must life turn dull, when
once it was so exciting? Why did love become a bore, when
it began so beautifully? Why is my job obnoxious when I
used to think it so worthwhile? And why have the things I
looked forward to become a disappointment? And most of
all, why is there death? Have I already experienced all there
is? Does a lifetime consist of a few years of happiness, every
now and then a noble deed, some fun with friends, some
pride in family, and in myself, and then that's it?

And the people I have loved, are they just gone? Can
nobody hope for anything more permanent than a street
named after them? Or a headstone with their name on it?
Or a single line in the ledger of the family heritage?

Will you help me with death, my mother? Oh, be beside
me, as you were beside your son, when loneliness piles up
in my heart because of the deaths of those I have loved.
And be extra care-full of me when the realization that I
must die shoots panic into my heart. Sometimes, Mary, my
lips want to tremble, as Jesus' did. I also want to scream out
against the enemy that threatens me with nothingness. I
want to shout "I thirst" as Jesus did. I thirst for life never to
end, for death never to swallow me up.

I thirst. I thirst for life. Amen.

### Prayer for Others

Mary, don't forget my family, my friends, and associates.
Death never comes easily, not for anyone. It is especially
difficult when it is a child who dies, or those starting out on
their education or careers, or those who were victims of
murder or any form of injustice.

Wherever they are, Mary, comfort those who grieve. You probably won't know what to say to them, any more than you knew what to say when you stood by the foot of the cross. Words never could manage the mystery of death. They never have, never will.

Never mind. Just be there for them, Mary. Let them understand how you were present for Jesus and how you stood up to death, even when you felt like saying, "I can't stand it."

You waited, as we wait now, for the world that came after the enemy. You went back to the upper room and helped the early Christians see things through until their Easter came.

Help us all to see it through. Make sure, my Lady, that we stand beside you and wait it out, through all the dying, then through death itself, and finally into life. Amen.

# *Sorrow Without Blinders*
## *Extra Sorrowful Mystery*

Jesus saw his mother standing beside the disciple whom Jesus loved. He said to his mother, "Woman, there is your Son." Then he said to his disciple, "There is your mother." And from that hour the disciple took her into his care.

John 19:25–27

The women who were with Jesus from Galilee saw the tomb and how his body was laid. Then they returned [to the upper room] and prepared spices. Then on the Sabbath day, they rested, according to the law.          Luke 23:53–56

### *Mary Speaks to You*
My friend, my beloved daughter, my cherished son, this is a personal favorite mystery of mine. It is a sorrow, cer-

tainly. But now that I look back on it, it was almost as joy-bearing an occasion as the birth of Christ. And it was almost, in a subdued fashion, as glorious as Pentecost.

I hope you realize that when Jesus said: "Behold your mother, behold your son," we celebrated our adoption ceremony right then and there. At the foot of the cross, with the last words Jesus said to any human, you all became my very own sons and daughters. John was the only one to hear it said directly of him, but he was everyone's representative in that regard. As you recall, Jesus did not speak to John as John. The words were addressed to "the disciple whom Jesus loved"; so they included everyone, because Jesus loves everyone. The words "Behold your mother" were directed to all the people Jesus loved and will love. No one has been left out.

And when my son called me by the diplomatic name of "woman" (not "Mom" or "Mother"), he was establishing me as the New Eve, *the* woman, united with him. I was the mother in a brand new kind of birth: one that brought forth children to new life.

"Woman," Jesus said to me, "behold your son, take care of him and all the sons and daughters I give you." Ever since then, you have been my sons and daughters—you, your loved ones, those you will meet in the future, the ones you like and the ones you don't like, everyone who will ever live are all my children.

That's why I can talk to you so easily, as though we were chatting at your kitchen table. I don't talk to you as lecturer, or counselor, or critic. I am your mother, and I love you very much.

Now think of me, that Good Friday afternoon, taking the slow walk back to the upper room. Think of the feelings I must have had. Apply to me your own most devastating trials—when your whole world seemed to cave in on you, and the person (or persons) you put your trust in were torn away from you, and life had no promise at all—no, none at all! That's how it was with me. I felt like sitting by the side of the road and weeping the rest of my life away. I wanted to scream out defiant shouts of anger against the injustice of it all. I was tempted to shake my fist at everyone, shun my friends, and insist on my right to feel sorry for myself.

After all, I did have the right to be miserable. My child had just died. Unjustly condemned. Dead at thirty-three. Too young to die. And he was innocent. Completely. He had not mistreated anyone. Not ever. Yet he was murdered by jealous, greedy rulers and by a crowd made up of cowards to the truth.

Crucified! Unjustly! Cruelly! If anyone had the right to rage against the apparent callousness of God for permitting such an atrocity, I had that right!

But you know I didn't use my right to express my outrage at the evil world. I had work to do. Jesus named me the mother of everyone, by that adoption ceremony at the cross. This meant all people for all time, but most immediately it meant that I must go back to the upper room and take care of the apostles and the women who would be waiting for me there.

It immediately struck me that I could not indulge the luxury of feeling sorry for myself. The disciples were so shaken by remorse, that they were almost destroyed. I had to comfort them. They were much more in need than I was. Their faith was not as strong as mine. Thank God, I could help them wait out those long, long hours until Easter. That grueling space of time between Good Friday afternoon and dawn on Sunday was a nightmare for us all. Yet it was a kind of nativity as well. When I helped Jesus' disciples stand fast against despair, I "gave birth" to them. They became my sons and daughters in a special way.

And I am here for you as well—as much a mother as I ever was. I am ready to reassure and support you when you are going through sufferings that seem unbearable, sorrows that conspire so strongly to take all hope away.

### *Prayer to Mary*

Blessed Mary, help me as you helped the Lord's first disciples. I know you were given to me to be my mother, so I call on you now and want to be sure I can call you in the future. I need you to be with me.

I get very down sometimes, and when I do, I tend to put blinders on my soul. You know how horses have blinders on so that they don't notice what is going on around them. The horse is ignorant of other horses, of its jockey, or the crowd, or anything. Nothing else exists, except what is straight ahead of them. Well, I've been like that. When some serious misfortune crushes me or a terrible injustice is done to me, I sometimes tend to tighten up on everything, not noticing anything in my world except my right to be hurt, or angry, or bitter. My grief wasn't nearly as great as yours, Mary, but it was something like it. I was the innocent victim of cruelty or grave misunderstanding. No doubt about it, I have suffered, and I have a right to feel hurt!

But I can't just quit on the rest of my life. Too many people depend on me. Too many people call me friend, a dependable member of my family, a good worker. These people are like the first disciples you adopted, Mary. They have a greater right to my affection, support, and love than I have a right to lose myself in self-pity.

Good Mother, gently lift the blinders from my eyes and heal my heartache. Show me how to notice other people again. Let me be open to the comfort I can get from friends, and the comfort that they can get from me. Amen.

### *Prayer for Others*

Blessed Mary, Mother of us all, comfort these people who have blinders on:

*(Here, mention those who are suffering from one of these experiences: the death of a dear one, mistreatment on the job or in the family, an affliction or a handicap, an unjustified and abrupt termination of a friendship—any other intervention that has so changed the person with sorrow that she or he is not alive to anything except the reasons for being embittered. Think of them in your prayer's center, but don't judge them. Don't become irritated because their bad attitudes are infecting the lives of those around them. Just tell Mary about their overwhelming sorrow and pray for their healing. And end your prayer like this:)*

Comfort them, dear Mother. Relieve the sickness of their souls. Help them as you did the first disciples; help them to wait it out. Give them a way to start noticing others who rely on them, and remind them that their sufferings will only last until God sees fit to replace all their afflictions with Easter Joy. Amen.

# Glorious Mysteries

# The Resurrection

After the Sabbath, toward the dawn of the day of the week, Mary, Mary Magdalene, and another woman went to see the tomb. But an angel said to the women, "Do not be afraid . . . Jesus has risen, as he said he would."     Matthew 28:1–10

## Mary Speaks to You

Jesus and I have a secret surrounding our reunion on Easter Sunday. We can't tell anybody about it. It's not that we refuse to be communicative. It's just that neither of us can find the right words for expressing what went on. The feelings are too awesome, too precious, too pure. How can anyone fit words to match the radiance of the first taste of heaven's glory?

You know how it is with the weaknesses of ordinary phrases. It's easy enough to talk about your times of joy. Happiness is meant to be shared, as best it can be. Sorrows, too, need solace. It's good to talk things out when you have pain. Hardly ever can healing happen without an understanding heart to hear your story. But glories? Those rare "moments of ecstasy"? Those experiences defy all attempts at accurate explanation.

Reread the different narratives about the Resurrection in each of the four gospels. They seem garbled. Staccato reports! Fumbling of words! There is even confusion among the actual eyewitnesses of the empty tomb. You see, the event was too spectacular, the effect on all the disciples was too exuberant for words. There couldn't be anything like a newspaper account of the Resurrection. It was impossible to be there and be a "detached observer."

We were all overwhelmed by the turnabout of life, of eternity, of everything.

Stunned awe, absolute victory over death, unassailable happiness forever, human love embracing divinity—all this was what we took part in when we began to understand that Jesus was truly raised from the tomb.

My son came to me before he greeted anybody else. Privately, just the two of us, as the first dim light of dawn caught the ridge of hills. Everyone was asleep. A certain instinct moved me to go to the well farthest from the buildings. I was drawing the bucket of water from the well when someone touched my hand to help me. I knew at once my son, my Lord, my Christ was there. We looked at each other. No words. I think I sighed. He smiled. His smile was larger than before—indeed, his "liveliness" was much larger than ever!

We embraced, and then we talked, somehow, and shared feelings. I don't remember exactly what we said. Anyway, that's our secret. I can tell you only this—the Prince Charming of all generations told me that I would be the heroine in all the folk tales of the world, and how, from then on, we would all live happily ever after. Not hopefully ever after, for hope is now a certainty. We shall live gloriously happy for all times.

And this is not just our folk tale, Jesus' and mine; now you belong to it as well. We all are one with him in his victory over death and over boredom and meanness and all the evil deeds anyone has ever done. We are united into his larger than life post-Easter paradise.

That is the essence of what we shared. I cannot say more about it. Our words belonged more to heaven than to earth. You will understand someday. Just keep holding on to the reality of Easter. Let hope be nourished by your unity with

Christ. Understanding will come slowly, as soon as prayer begins, at last, to understand.

## *Prayer to Mary*

Thank you, Blessed Mary, for being honest about your secrets. I know something of what you mean. I have had my moments of exuberant happiness, intimate expressions of love, explosions of beauty and significance; these events still belong to me. They are the rare times that are the best times of my life.

There were not too many of them, but I remember them very well:

*(Here, list the glories in your life. In your own way, tell Mary about those times when life was most exhilarating: when you fell in love, achieved a moment of notoriety in school, in sports, in your job, experienced the physical/spiritual ecstasy of married union, wondered at the sight of your baby, felt the thrill of doing the right thing, being in the right place, saying the right words. Mention all other experiences in your life that allow you to say in your heart, "Yes, I am grateful for the moments that have made me feel so good about myself; I am glad, very glad, I was born!")*

You know these times of my life already, Mary. You and Jesus understood the secrets of my greatest glories. I cannot share them with anyone else. The memory of them still amazes me; they can be cherished only in the silence of prayer. I'm glad I was given these good memories. They help me to hope for even greater happiness when I die and begin to live with Jesus on the other side of silence.

Bless me, Mary. Stay very close to me. Sometimes other memories come to my mind—the darker ones—those saddening events that still try to convince me that I'm no good, not worth anybody's notice, or incapable of having any chance for living happily . . . ever! Please don't let those bad experiences master me. Let me call to mind your ultimate success, shared in secret, when Jesus gave you the life of God, making it possible for you to live forever after . . . happily. Amen.

### *Prayer for Others*

Blessed Mary, by the Easter mystery that gives honor to your heaven-grounded happiness, I pray for all lonely people who are in the world, especially for those living in the part of the world I know the best, my own. Many people have to keep to themselves their times of greatest glory. They can't tell anyone about the happiest moments in their lives, or share their most wonderful accomplishments. It seems that they never stop talking about their sickness, worries, and all their other woes. They go on and on with their hurt feelings, old ailments, financial burdens. But they hardly ever speak about the best that is in them—their noble moments in the past, their deeds of unselfish love that they should be so proud of.

Shyness is one reason they seldom speak about their good side. So many people have been trained not to glory in their achievements, or tell people what has already happened in their lives that deserves honest praise. Another reason for not speaking up is your reason, too, my Lady. Words don't come easy when you try to give adequate expression to things that have deep-down significance. You find the words for them, Mary—words they can share quietly with you.

Don't let them be bullied by negative memories—about what is wrong, or worrisome, or distressing. The constant input of these memories will destroy all possibility of prayer. Help them to go back to their best secrets, to their most exhilarating moments. And from these, let them be prepared for the fullest, most radiant secret of them all: the life your son *eastered* for the whole world taught us all to wait, with hope, for the happy outcome of eternity. Amen.

# *The Ascension*

The disciples went to Galilee. . . . Jesus said to them, "All power has been given to me. Go, therefore, preach the gospel and make disciples of all nations . . . and remember I am with you always, even to the end of the world."
Matthew 28:18–20; Mark 16:15

### *Mary Speaks to You*

My dear friend, in Matthew's Gospel you will learn the right way to say goodbye. At least you will learn the way Jesus said goodbye to us. When he ascended to heaven, we all knew that the leave-taking marked the end of how life used to be.

It was not like the end of things as in death. Not that at all. Death had already been killed on Easter Sunday. It was as if Jesus was going on a long journey and God alone knew when we would catch up to him.

Jesus' words were powerful, when the time for his farewell came. There was a formal element to the occasion. It seemed as though we all took part in a graduation exercise. Yes, we are graduating, with solemn rites. All the disciples—my sons and daughters now—were entering into their new life with fresh enthusiasm. They were fully matured, fully trained, at last. It was wonderful to see them conducting themselves with Christ-like confidence . . . *and* acceptance. The scene had everything but the diplomas and caps we could fling in the air.

Our Lord's words served as the baccalaureate address. The difference between this graduation and others was that *this* honorary speaker did not just *urge* the graduates to achieve success; Jesus was actually giving them the *power* and *authority* to achieve it.

As a matter of fact, "power" was the key word in the address. God had given the Word-made-flesh all power—that is, all authority, competence, and energy—and now he handed it over to all of us. "Get going," Jesus told us. "Go where I send you and give the people an ever-increasing dose of life, confidence, and hope. And remember," said my son, and these were the last words he spoke, "Remember I am with you, always, as long as life shall last."

I am with you! What a beautiful way to say goodbye. Of course, that phrase reminded me of our beginnings. The Christmas Angel told my husband, in his dream, to name my child Emmanuel because Jesus was living proof of how tenderly God is with us. Jesus will always be the proof that God is with us. After the graduation, when the Lord was taken up to the heavens, his spirit was just as alive to us as when he walked about in Galilee. The disciples were living witnesses, especially in the way they lived, making believable the fact that God was love and that God's love was real. Christ's power over death was certainly majestic. His creative life and joy will last forever. We came to learn this more deeply as we recalled the words and deeds of Jesus and the way we loved one another.

With Christ's farewell that day, the last part of God's glorious love-drama was in place; the divine gifts of benevolence and compassion were complete. How can anyone—since then—ever doubt the destiny of love? How can you

ever doubt it? How can any siege of depression or temptation to despair overcome such pledges to your faith? How
can you even conceive that death is the end of everything?

Our Lord is with us. Long after death has done its deed,
Jesus will be with us still. That's what it means to graduate
with Christ. That's how Jesus blessed us then, and blesses
us now. That's how he so gloriously said goodbye!

### *Prayer to Mary*

Blessed Mary, please don't let me be hurt by too much
loneliness. I know it can't be helped sometimes. Everyone
must be bored and lonely now and again, but feeling too
much alone and for too long can be devastating.

I find goodbyes hard to manage. When someone has to
leave me because of death or a distant assignment or for
some other reason, let the life and the love we shared be a
gift we both can keep. Somehow, let what we were together continue to be part of each of us.

There are other kinds of loneliness too. Sometimes, Mary,
these pull me down. I get an empty feeling when suddenly
it is life itself that seems hollow to me. I become strangely
disgusted with what I do and what I am and how little I
have accomplished compared to how much I wanted to
achieve. There are times when I feel as though I've said
goodbye to myself, and don't want to face myself any more!

Heal me of these ugly graduations, Mary. Help me to
remember what Jesus meant by *power*—when he gave that
wonderful energy-of-life to his disciples. God's power is
the creative spark that gives zest to friendship, meaning to
work, and joy to life. Let me remember all I have enjoyed in
life and make sure I never deny the best of what I am simply because I sometimes feel empty and worthless.

And finally, Mary, be a good mother to me when I feel

lonely, distant from God. When darkness has replaced the consolation and light I experience at times of prayer, when my wrongdoing has made me feel alienated or lacking in faith, then comfort me, my Lady, and give me peace. Let me know in my heart-of-hearts that Jesus is still Emmanuel, still lives up to his name, is still with us. And, Mary, please be an Emmanuel for me yourself. Amen.

### *Prayer for Others*

Blessed Mary, I make my most earnest appeal for all who suffer from these forms of loneliness. I pray especially for those who are lonely to themselves, who are disgusted with the way they live . . . or who grieve too much and too inconsolably for their lost loves . . . or who have become embittered because they lack money or have missed opportunities.

*(Here, mention people you know who suffer from these misfortunes. Pray to Mary in your own words for as long as it seems right to you.)*

Please, Blessed Mother, don't let them snap. See to it that they remember whatever is good in them, and whatever good they have done. Please touch them with these uplifting thoughts, and encourage them to accept the gifts of life and energy that you received when your son ascended to heaven.

His farewell was a promise to *be with*; his leave-taking was the pledge of life; his goodbye was sacred to the memory of your shared love.

Help those who feel isolated right now to understand that maybe their present barrenness is one way to be with the Lord. Their barrenness or bitterness won't last forever.

A change will surely come, one day. Commencement exercises will begin before the whole world sinks.

Give them this hope, Mary. Turn their aloneness into an awareness of Christ's last blessing . . . and with his first disciples, let us all unite with three cheers for Jesus Christ on our graduation day. Amen.

# *The Holy Spirit's Appearance*

[After the Ascension of the Lord,] the apostles returned to Jerusalem . . . and with one mind they continued steadfastly in prayer with the women and with Mary, the mother of Jesus. . . . When Pentecost came, they were all together in one place, and suddenly there came a sound from heaven, and there appeared tongues, looking like fire, which settled on each of them. And they were all filled with the Holy Spirit and began to speak . . . to Parthians and Medes and Elamites and inhabitants of Mesopotamia and Cappadocia and Asia and Egypt and Libya and Rome . . . speaking to all, in their own languages, about the wonderful things God does. Acts 1:12—2:12

## *Mary Speaks to You*

If you look carefully at most of the nativity scenes you see around Christmas time, you'll notice that I'm not alone with my baby. With Joseph and me, there are usually a flock of shepherds and a few wise men and sometimes angels in the sky. The birth of the Messiah was never intended to be an unwitnessed solitary event.

It's the same idea with the second birthday of salvation we call Pentecost. There were a lot of people taking part in the amazing phenomenon. Everyone was there to amplify amazement over God's powerful gift of life.

I want to keep coming back to the word "power." If you don't get a profound feel for this word, you won't get a sense for what happened on that first Pentecost and you'll be missing out on the joy that God wants you to experience.

The angel of the Lord told me, right in the beginning at the annunciation, to "wait . . . and the power from on high will overshadow you." The divine energy of all created things will be the energy that will make me pregnant with the Word of God. The power from on high did this for me . . . and that same power is available for you.

People have been used to calling the third person of the Blessed Trinity by the name Holy Ghost, or Holy Spirit. Okay, use "Holy Spirit" if you are comfortable with it. But remember the gospel significance of those other words that serve as metaphors. God is the energy of God, the capacity for life and understanding, and especially the power of God.

If you think of divine attributes in terms of *power*, in contrast to weakness or ineffectiveness, and *energy*, as opposed to listlessness, you can understand why Pentecost can be called a new nativity. At the annunciation, God's message was only for me. I was told to wait for power coming from on high. At the ascension, Christ's message was given to all the men, women, and children who were the first members of the early church. Jesus gave them the same message I received over thirty years before. "Wait," Jesus told them, "until you are clothed with power from on high!"

And then the power came. It was a wonderful feeling to be a part of that exuberant occasion. The excitement sparkled all over. Gratitude for God's plan of love was in everyone's heart and prompted the words that expressed our great wonder. Thousands of people heard us all at once—with each one praising God in a different language.

The whole world's gratitude was offered back to God.
Everyone there was caught up in the stories of God's new
ways with creatures.

At Jesus' birth, angels said, "Glory to God in the highest!"
At Pentecost, it was we who had the impetus—the human
impetus—to sing "Glory to the Great Energy of God"!

### *Prayer to Mary*

Blessed Mary, I have to shift a bit in the way I visualize
you. In those holy pictures I've looked at since my youth,
you are mostly sad—either grieving over the death of your
son, caused by our sins, or disappointed in us because of
our misbehavior or lack of prayer. Even when you look loving, you have only a half-smile on your face as you present
your child to the adoring shepherds. I've never heard you
laughing, or shouting for sheer joy, or expressing yourself
with such an infectious mixture of praise and laughter that
all who were listening to you from Macedonia, Libya, India,
and Rome were able to catch fire by the fire you were filled
with.

Mary, help me be touched by your charm and exhilara-
tion. And from the way I share in your profound gratitude,
let me learn to encourage others to be upbeat too. Part of me
wants to drag my feet through life—even to shun parties or
get-togethers—although, in my heart, I know that celebrations and congratulations are called for.

*(Here, mention certain glad occasions that have come up in the
last few years: a cookout planned to praise a child for excellence at
school or in sports; a party to congratulate someone on their promotion or other grand achievement; the retirement of a neighbor
or family member; a wedding feast; a move into a new house, to a
new town, or a new position; a christening party. Whatever gen-*

*erates joyful excitement about life and gives credit somehow to the energy of love. Think about these things as events somewhat similar to Pentecost. Taking as much time as seems good to you, tell Mary about them in your own words. Then continue your prayer.)*

Mary, sometimes I hold back from such invitations to celebrate life. It could be that I'm jealous of other people's good fortune. It could be that I'm busy with my own preoccupations. It could be that I think of the future, the times that come after celebrations are over, and I worry about unknown prospects around the corner.

Don't let me be a killjoy, Mary. Sure, you knew the apostles would suffer because they were linked to Christ. Most of them would be martyred. But that didn't stop you from feeling the full measure of expansive joy at Pentecost. That was the time for shared delight—so you took part in it. It was a day to revel in love's energy, right to the brim.

Let me be a part of your gladness, then and now. Let me be active in sharing the good news: whenever the time and whatever the place for sharing it. Give me the willingness to find energy in all our continued Pentecosts. Amen.

### *Prayer for Others*

Blessed Mary, now I pray for those especially who cannot feel the energy of love, or the power of life. They have died to hope and they shun the celebrations of family and friends.

*(Here, without making judgments, name those who suffer because they refuse to rejoice over the success, good fortune, or fresh prospects of others. They have become so soured on people, they cannot feel the effects of Pentecost in any form. In your own*

*words and with the spirit of compassion, tell our Lady about their unhappiness.)*

Help them, Blessed Mary. Get them to see you as you were that Pentecost morning with your gift of tongues. Put enough hope into them that they can begin to give gratitude a chance. At the very least, help them to feel grateful for other people's gifts, if not their own. Amen.

# The Patience of Pentecost
### Extra Glorious Mystery

[After men, women, and children from different countries had given expression to the great deeds God had done,] Peter stood and lifted up his voice and spoke to all the people there assembled.                                    Acts 2:7–14

### Mary Speaks to You

There was another side to Pentecost that deserves a decade of the rosary all to itself. It wasn't much of a happy experience, but it was a part of God's glorious takeover of the world. So the patience I displayed on Pentecost deserves a place in your prayer.

I was shocked into silence that memorable morning after having such a wonderful time praising God in languages I never knew before. I was not exactly shunned by Simon Peter, or shunted off; I was simply sidelined. Peter took full charge of the events. Center stage suddenly passed me by.

Nobody's fault. Responsibilities just drain away, little by little, as you get older. All people discover that situations come up when they are no longer as qualified as they used to be. Even though I understood it was Simon Peter's role to silence everybody that morning and be the one and only voice to explain what had happened, it was still difficult to let go of control. What I was doing was so satisfying: giving glory to Jesus' victory over death and his gift of everlasting life, being energized by the languages of love that I spoke. After all my grieving during Holy Week, waiting for my son's rare appearances through the Easter season, it was so good to simply lean back and take it all in as the praise of God swelled up from my heart. Not since I sang my Magnificat when I visited my cousin Elizabeth did I feel as exhilarated about my faith as I did on Pentecost.

Then I had to quiet down. We all did. Andrew confessed to me, afterward, that he was tempted to shout his brother Peter down. For a moment, something in him wanted to blurt out: "No! Peter, I won't shut up! I've got as much right to praise the wonderful works of God as you have! And besides, even though I fell asleep on Jesus and ran away on him, at least I didn't deny him the way you did! So don't silence me, Peter, just because you want to be the one to talk to everybody. Let's keep this sacred event going just the way it is!"

Well, Andrew resisted that temptation, of course. Even so, I could understand how he felt. You can too, I guess. Everyone registers heartfelt regret when life somehow passes them by. The child is sad when he puts away his toys and starts to go to school. The teenager remembers wistfully a time when summers meant just playing and not holding down a job. Class reunions carry the mood of the good old days that once were so carefree. And retirement, being put on the shelf for one reason or another, most closely resembles what I went through, that late Pentecost morning.

The world has passed you by, some whisper told me.

"Things don't get done the way they did before. Somebody else is running things. Simon Peter is spokesman for the church; he's the glue that will put sacred history together. You're on the sidelines now."

You know how it is. I know you know. That's why I brought it up. I understand what's going on with you. I've been there. So you can tell me all about it and count on my comforting assurance.

### *Prayer to Mary*

Blessed Mary, I marvel at the different ways you speak to me. It's good to know I can lay bare my embarrassing secrets. I have this fear of being shoved aside by those who promise— or threaten—to replace me. Call it my replacement sadness. These are the situations that bother me the most.

*(Here, present in your own words whatever makes you feel let down: your spouse, children, or other family members changing the way they think of you, your hunch that now they take you for granted, your complaint that they don't bother to include you in what they do; fellow workers who now go over your head, or go around you, when they want important things done, or who get the best assignments [the most challenging, the most lucrative] that you used to get; friends who share secrets with one another, but not with you; retiring from work or just plain slowing down. Mention any other situation forcing you to step aside, step down, or leave. Tell Mary, in a way that's right for you, how hurt you are, how your world is wrenched away from you, a world you thought would never change.)*

Please, Mary, be with me when I'm on the sidelines watching the parade beginning to pass me by. It's hard to talk about these things with friends or family. Sometimes, they're part of the problem. Sometimes I'm afraid they wouldn't understand. They would lecture me, and lectures I don't need! They'd tell me to stop worrying and give me advice.

But I don't want advice. I don't need to be told how letting go is part of life. I just wanted someone who went through the same feelings and will hear me out when I'm down in the dumps.

You're such a someone, Blessed Mother. You are such a friend. After your highs of Easter and Pentecost, you had to take a back seat too. Let me be content with the gifts I still have and the opportunities to use them. And, with you beside me, let me grow in wisdom; don't let me just grow old. Amen.

### Prayer for Others

Blessed Mary, I pray especially 1) for those of any age who suffer serious illness. Suddenly they must be on the sidelines of active life. That hurts. 2) For those who have recently retired. It's difficult to give up control and let others take over. To lose one's dynamism is almost like admitting defeat. It's not easy. They don't always take retirement in the best grace. They need your help. 3) And for everyone who cares for these people: the nurses and doctors, the family and visiting friends. They really need your lessons of patience and your experience of helping people to let go.

Mary, as you know, people resent the fact that they are no longer as useful as they once were. Age, debility, preference for someone else on the job, dirty politics, or even (as in your case, Mary) stepping aside for someone else, like Peter, to take charge of things—any of these changes can come as a shock. Please, Mary, assure them that all is well when they do what they can, even though they sometimes grumble about it.

Help them with patience. Be with them just as you were with the apostle Andrew—who was told by his brother to quiet down—and was put on the sidelines of the first Pentecost excitement. Help everyone when it becomes someone else's job to tell the crowd about the way their future will unfold. Amen.

# *The Assumption*

Jesus said, "A woman about to give birth is sorrowful, because her time has come. But when she has brought forth her child, joy makes her forget her anguish because life has come into the world. So I will see you again, and your hearts shall rejoice, and your joy no one will take away from you."

John 16:20–22

### *Mary Speaks to You*

It was amazing how quickly I became accustomed to my new life in heaven. It was as though everything in my nature had always presumed that this was the way to live. Then I started to live it.

I died somewhere north of Judea. St. John took care of me all through my last years. Then, when I died, he put me in an unmarked tomb, which no one had ever used. My death came during a peaceful afternoon nap. Then I was transported, somehow, to this sacred place. Honestly, I don't know how it all happened. Even if I asked Jesus to describe it to you, he couldn't do it satisfactorily, either. It would be easier to explain to a child what happens when a baby is born than to explain how I got here.

Yes, I'm living in heaven now, totally and perfectly. "Assumed" into heaven is the fancy word for it. What it means is that I am all here, soul and body—my son and I are the only "all here" humans in heaven so far.

Don't get me wrong. Everyone who has died in faith and all those who lived a trusting "yes" to life according to their sincere persuasions are here in heaven as well. But there's still the matter of their resurrection to experience, their bodies being joined once more to their souls. This will take place at the end of time.

How are all these people living? How am I living? How does the God-man Jesus live with both of his natures functioning? How will you live out eternity, once you get here?

To all four questions, "No comment!" Just take it on faith that Christ spoke the truth when he promised the full-future for all people. He has told you in so many words: "The moment you die, you will be born to a brand new way of life that's just as mysteriously different as the change that happened to you the first time. When you were a baby in your mother's womb, you were alive, all right, alive for nine whole months. But for those months, your style of life, you must admit, was quite a cramped existence. Not much was going on. You were unable to think, or see things, or have friends, or understand stories, or laugh at jokes. You were just 'alive and kicking.' Then out you came and soon your life was much richer, fuller, wiser, more capable of happiness, and certainly much more complex.

"Well, when you come through your second birth by dying to your familiar world and joining us in heaven, you'll experience a quantum leap of life-style even greater than the one that happened when you were born the first time. Here, in heaven, life is richer than it ever was on earth."

My son told you that. He promised it when he consoled his disciples, the night before he died. He compared himself to a mother giving birth, and then, after the anguish of Good Friday, he said, "I will be the kind of mother who is

radiant with joy because I have brought about a Godlike
existence for all people. And when this existence becomes
your ordinary way of life, you'll feel a joy that no one and
nothing shall ever take from you!"

That hint is really all you will ever know about heaven—
until you get here. Even so, Christ's words should be
enough for you. Your work, while still on earth, is to stay
with it and pray yourself into the hope of it. Don't forget the
consolation of those words: "No one will ever take away
your joy." That is, no person, no situation, no sickness, no
act of cruelty or thoughtlessness, no financial or family burdens, no hurt from anything. Think about it. Draw up a list,
ten thousand items long, of all the individuals, hardships,
pains, embarrassments, lack of anything, whatever has made
you sad or lonely or inoperative or puzzled or frustrated.
Then write a second list of little things that have upset your
life: thoughtlessness among shoppers, misunderstandings
among friends, obnoxious drivers, things like that. Not one
of these will ever be seen, felt, or known in heaven.

Isn't that wonderful? Now think of all those things that
have made you happy. Remember an evening out with
friends, Christmas, a particularly festive wedding, other
great times with family; recall the promotion you got, the
scholarship, the high marks or a teacher's praise, the touch-
down you scored; remember the first time you fell in love,
saved a life, praised a child, proved your loyalty to a friend,
were asked to join an organization you wanted to belong to,
and how good you felt. That is, think of everything you
have cherished, in one way or another, even to the pet kit-
ten you had, or that special little space you went to when
you were little. Well, Jesus promises you that all of this will
be present somehow. All will be a part of your joy that no
one will ever take away from you.

Somehow. All I can promise is somehow. Don't you try to imagine how. The ties of love and friendship, the best of all the wisdom and expertise you have been blessed with, all this will still be real. But they will not be lived with in the same way. Don't try to invent images about what it will be like. Don't ask experts or trust anyone's claim in this regard. You can no more understand how we live here in heaven than an unborn baby can conceive of what life will be like when she grows up.

You'll just have to wait until you die and get here. I know the way you must travel. Let me banish your doubts; let me guide you on your journey; and let me greet you when you get here, which, please God, you will.

### Prayer to Mary

Thank you, Blessed Mary. You've given me much comfort. It's good that I don't have to leave everything behind when I die. I will live on in the hearts of those who love me. And I will confidently wait for those who will die after me.

It does me good, my Lady, to think of those I love who have died. I'm so glad I don't have to think of them as vague shadowy forms, or impassive memories that become dimmer and dimmer as the days go on. I know they are real, with real ways of communicating. I know I can't understand exactly how they do this or how they register their joy, but they remember me and they thank God for their wonderful life.

Jesus really meant what he said, and he is good for the happiness he promised. If I can't believe him, I can't believe anybody. Just show me your mother's love, Mary, when I'm scared by the thought of what I don't know . . . and scared by death. Please be with me when I get lonely because so many people I have loved have left me. Be with me, gentle woman, with the confidence of your assumption and with the vitality of that trust in God you had throughout all the years you lived on earth before your son "gave birth" to you in heaven. Amen.

### *Prayer for Others*

Glorious Lady, give consolation to the dying. Be their assurance and their guide to the new home made possible by Jesus. And give special comfort to those who grieve the dead. I remember how innocent children were murdered in Bethlehem, soon after your child was born. Matthew's gospel tells how the families mourned so much they refused to be consoled. I'm sure they hated you, too, and hated God as well because their loss was connected to the life of your baby. Yet the birth of Jesus ultimately meant the everlasting life of those children who were murdered.

Blessed Mary, I know some people—young and old—who are angry at God because of the death of a dear one. Please help them consider your assumption to heaven. Reach them so that they don't turn away from God and give up on life. Put their sorrow in a cup and drink it for them, and get them to understand how, although their loved ones died to the first two worlds they lived in—the world of their mother's womb and then of the mother-earth—they now have entered into the final world prepared for them for all eternity . . . where they no longer drink from their cups of sorrow, but share, with you and all the saints, the chalice of perfect joy. Amen.

# The Coronation

One day Jesus got into the boat with his disciples . . . and a great storm of wind arose and the waves were beating into the boat. . . . The apostles said to Jesus, "Save us, Lord; we are perishing!" Then Jesus rebuked the wind and said to the sea, "Peace! Be Still!" and the wind ceased and there was a great calm.     Matthew 8:23–27; Mark 4:35–41; Luke 8:22–25

## Mary Speaks to You

With all our means of investigation, all the news-reporting staffs and TV satellites, it's becoming more and more difficult to hang on to heroes, isn't it? No sooner do you become a part of the cult of worship of an athlete, astronaut, movie star, millionaire, or promising politician . . . than down falls the star into the dust of controversy. For a time, you felt good about identifying yourself with his or her success. Your aspirations, at least some of them, became melded into the charm, power, or mass appeal of your hero. And it all went well . . . for a while. Then it vanished into thin air. You are stuck with make-believe, or you grieve over "what used to be," or else you turn sour on all performers of great accomplishments because you had reached for a star that turned out to be a cinder!

Cynicism can run wild after heroes fall. I don't want you to lose heart. My son and I are still the heroes you can count on. Find the spring-in-your-step that children have. That is what Jesus meant when he said that children are the citizens of the Kingdom. Return to the childlike capacity for awe and wonder; enter into stories of noble deeds and living happily ever after.

My last mystery of the rosary reminds you of the unconquerable vitality of human hopes. For ages, people have called this mystery my "queenship." I am portrayed as being honored with a solemn coronation, sitting beside my son, who is Christ the King.

Fine. These terms of royalty make sense to a lot of people. But many more find the words "king "and "queen" confusing. Too uppity, too far removed from ordinary life. If you feel this way, call us heroes, instead. Jesus and I are real folk heroes, you know. You can look up to us, follow right along with us, and model your life on what you see and hear from us. After all, that is what you do with other heroes. We are the two who won't let you down.

Some heroes do. Jesus never will! He has the power over the winds and waves that threaten to sweep you overboard. With him by your side, injustices or deprivations won't overwhelm you; neither will anxieties . . . not even death itself.

Consider my son as your hero, then. And include me also as the hero of your hopes. Sports figures will die away on you. Movie stars fade so that only the very old remember them. Millionaires go broke, or go to jail. Pop stars may choke. Debutantes age and become pudgy as time goes on. That's life—when you consider only life on earth. Either time erodes, or scandals tarnish, the people you pinned your hopes on.

Then only two of us are left. But two are enough to provide you with everything you need in order to live as best you can right now. And we can guide you to the kingdom where fairy tales make perfect sense—where I am your Godmother, Jesus is your Prince Charming, and you live happily forever . . . without a tear or worry in the world.

### *Prayer to Mary*
Mary, kind Mother, Blessed Queen, faithful hero of mine:

help me to switch gears. I know you don't want me to stop admiring those people who are gifted with outstanding qualities or noteworthy achievement. But I must never surround them with an aura of hero-worship. They have, like all humans, only feet of clay.

Here, at the last prayers of your rosary, Mary, let me remember Jesus in that boat on Lake Galilee, ringed about with menacing waves. Let me imagine that all the elements of storm surrounding the frail vessel represent the many furies that threaten me at times. Let the violence of wind and the drowning power of waves be the anxieties and grief that have menaced me. Worries are the winds blowing me off course. Depression is the pounding of wave after wave, trying to capsize me.

Help me place my hand into the steady hands of my forever-hero. Jesus will bring me safely home. And you, my comforter, my queen, will see to it that I am in a secure haven at last. Then, when I go from this life to the next, I can say I've lived in the only true folk tale that has passed the test of time. I have given witness to heroics in the most majestic setting imaginable . . . forever grateful . . . forever after. Amen. Alleluia.

### *Prayer for Others*

And now, Blessed Mary, I pray for all those who have asked my help and my prayers. In a special way I pray for those who have turned their backs to the world . . . caused hope to go sour . . . become cynical critics because of tarnished heroes, or crashed ideals, or disappointed loves. Heal them of their unhappiness, my Lady. Get them to notice you and your son. Don't let them snuff out all of life because they put too much expectation into some fragile parts of it.

You and Jesus are the only ones who can stand the test of time. That's why you are the ideal king and queen. That's why you're real heroes.

Tell that to those who need healing. They are grieving too much. They will sink if they aren't rescued soon. Get them to return to their childhood—the happy side of their childhood—and discover again that hope is possible. Then suggest that they begin to pin these hopes on you and Jesus and all that Jesus promised. And then they will finally get it right. Amen.

There are other people I have meant to pray for, too. I promised them a rosary, at least in my own mind. And even though they have slipped my mind . . . or I somehow failed to mention them . . . I do love them. I wish them the blessings of your comfort and the courage of your hero-son. Take care of them for me. I know you will. Amen.

Good night, Mother.